FIGURE SKATING

BY ASHLEY GISH

CREATIVE EDUCATION · CREATIVE PAPERBACKS

Published by Creative Education and Creative Paperbacks
P.O. Box 227, Mankato, Minnesota 56002
Creative Education and Creative Paperbacks are imprints of
The Creative Company
www.thecreativecompany.us

Design by The Design Lab
Production by Rachel Klimpel
Art direction by Rita Marshall
Printed in the United States of America

Photographs by Alamy (PCN Photography, SPUTNIK, Taka Wu,
Xinhua), AP Images (ASSOCIATED PRESS), Dreamstime (Franco
Ricci), Getty Images (MCT/Tribune News Service), iStockphoto
(Artur Didyk), Shutterstock (Diego Barbieri, Nicholas Piccillo, abozzi
tonello, Victoria VIAR PRO)

Library of Congress Cataloging-in-Publication Data
Names: Gish, Ashley, author.
Title: Figure skating / Ashley Gish.
Series: Amazing Winter Olympics.
Includes bibliographical references and index.
Summary: Celebrate the Winter Games with this high-interest
introduction to figure skating, the sport known for its singles, pairs,
and ice dancing events. Also included is a biographical story about
figure skater Yuzuru Hanyu.

Identifiers:
ISBN 978-1-64026-494-6 (hardcover)
ISBN 978-1-68277-046-7 (pbk)
ISBN 978-1-64000-624-9 (eBook)
This title has been submitted for CIP processing under LCCN
2021937334.

Table of Contents

Figure skating became part of the Summer Olympic Games in 1908. In 1924, the sport moved to the Winter Games. Herma Szabo, from Austria, won the gold medal in women's skating then.

Russians Ludmila Belousova and Oleg Protopopov took gold twice in the 1960s.

Events in Olympic figure skating

include men's singles, women's singles, pairs, and ice dancing. A man and a woman are partners in pairs skating and ice dancing. But there are a few differences between these two events.

Ice dancers must always stay within two arms' lengths of each other during a skate.

Pairs skating involves jumps and spins. The man may lift or throw his partner into the air. Ice dancers do not do this. Instead, they focus on their steps and **rhythm**.

rhythm a pattern of sounds and movement

Skate guards are plastic covers that protect the blades when a skater is off the ice.

Figure skaters wear skates made for this sport. The blades are longer and heavier than hockey skate blades. Skaters use the **toe picks** on each skate to grip the ice as they prepare to jump.

toe picks sawlike teeth at the front tip of a figure skating blade

Skaters often wear sparkly outfits made just for them. Crystals are applied by hand. Some skaters attach a good-luck charm to their outfit. Skaters lose points if these pieces fall onto the ice.

Competitors show their feelings through facial expressions and body movements.

FIGURE SKATING

Judges give two sets of points. The technical score is based on how hard the skater's program is. This includes spins and jumps. The axel is one of the most difficult jumps. A triple axel means the skater turns around in the air three and a half times before landing.

Olympic skating programs have become harder over the years.

The program component score is for creativity and style. The event winner is the skater or pair with the most points.

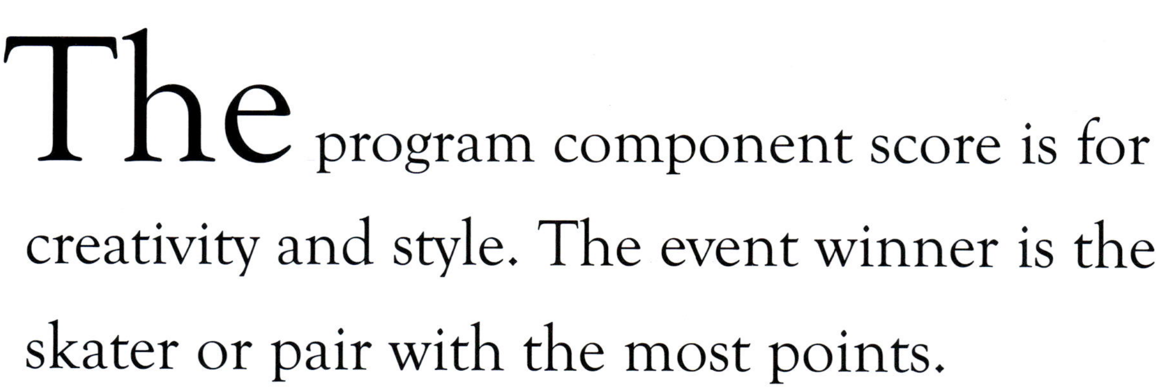

Skating partners practice together many hours a day to build trust in each other.

Shen and Zhao won bronze in 2002 and 2006 before earning gold in 2010.

Russian competitors hold the longest **winning streak** in Olympic figure skating. Russian figure skating pairs won gold every time they competed from 1964 until 2006. China's Shen Xue and Zhao Hongbo broke Russia's streak in 2010.

winning streak a series of wins occurring one right after another

Skaters glide gracefully across the ice. They complete dizzying spins. They launch themselves into amazing jumps. Millions of people watch this popular sport during the Winter Olympics.

Figure skaters are graceful and athletic, making difficult moves look easy.

Competitor Spotlight: Yuzuru Hanyu

Yuzuru Hanyu

is a men's figure skater from Sendai, Japan. In 2011, he was practicing at an ice rink in his hometown. Suddenly, an earthquake shook the arena. Yuzuru overcame the disaster and skated for Japan at the 2014 Winter Olympics. He won gold as Japan's first champion figure skater. He claimed another gold medal at the 2018 Games in Pyeongchang, South Korea.

Read More

Hunter, Nick. *The Winter Olympics*. Chicago: Heinemann, 2014.

Ventura, Marne. *STEM in Figure Skating*. Minneapolis: SportsZone, 2018.

Waxman, Laura Hamilton. *Figure Skating*. North Mankato, Minn.: Amicus, 2018.

Websites

Kiddle: Figure Skating Facts for Kids
https://kids.kiddle.co/Figure_skating
Learn more about jumps, spins, turns, and steps.

Liveaboutdotcom: Figure Skating Olympic Champions
https://www.liveabout.com/olympic-figure-skating-women-gold
-medalists-1282784
Read more about figure skating gold medalists.

Index